Little K...
Big Cat

Contents

Rigby

Just Born!

A mother cat feeds and
cleans her kittens.
She doesn't need help to care
for her kittens.
But she does need special care
for herself.

How Do I Care for a Mother Cat?

- Give her plenty of water.

- Give her food.

- Keep her bed in a warm place.

Cat Facts

A kitten will open its eyes at about ten days.

A kitten will hear at two weeks.

A kitten will walk at three weeks.

Two Months

Now a kitten
can leave its mother.
It can go to a new home.

How Do I Care for a Two-Month-Old Kitten?

- Give the kitten a soft bed.

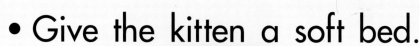

- Give the kitten a clean litter box.

- Give the kitten food and water three times a day.

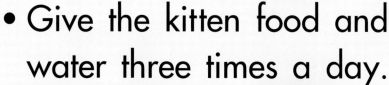

A kitten uses its tongue to clean its fur.

A kitten's eyes will change color at two months.

A kitten's baby teeth
will fall out at six months.

Six Months

Kittens love to play.
Make your house safe
for the playful kitten.
Put locks on doors
so the kitten won't get
into dangerous things.
Put rubber bands
and string in jars
so the kitten won't eat them.

How Do I Care for a Six-Month-Old Kitten?

- Give the kitten food and water two times a day.

- Make sure the house is safe.

- Brush the kitten's fur with a special brush.

Some kittens have long hair.

Some kittens have short hair.

Some kittens do not have a tail!

Some kittens do not have any hair!

Nine Months

The kitten has learned to show how it feels. Sometimes the kitten hisses when it is afraid. When it rubs against you, it is saying, "I love you!"

Hissss!

How Do I Care for a Nine-Month-Old Kitten?

- Give the kitten food and water two times a day.

- Give the kitten a larger litter box.

- Clean the kitten's ears.

A kitten's tongue is rough.

A kitten likes to sleep
in sunny places.

A kitten can turn its ears.

All Grown Up!

When a kitten is one year old,
it is an adult cat.
The cat is now strong and
can have kittens of its own.

How Do I Care for an Adult Cat?

- Make sure the cat's fur is clean.

- Make sure the cat's claws are not too long.

- Clean the cat's teeth.

Cat Facts

Cats can run fast.
They can jump high.
But they still need people
to love and care for them!

How Big Is a Kitten?

Age

Newborn

Two Months

Six Months

Nine Months

One Year

Weight

How Heavy Is That?

4 ounces	
2 pounds	
5 pounds	
10 pounds	
12 pounds	

Index

How big is a kitten?
22

How do I feed a cat?
3, 7, 11, 15

How do I keep a kitten safe?
10

How do I keep a cat clean?
8, 11, 15, 19

What does a cat like to do?
10

What kinds of cats are there?
12-13